Forward into Light:
The Struggle for Woman's Suffrage
edited by Madeleine Meyers

© Discovery Enterprises, Ltd.
Lowell, Massachusetts
1994

© Discovery Enterprises, Ltd., Lowell, MA 1994

ISBN 1-878668-25-0 paperback edition
Library of Congress Catalog Card Number 93-70436

10   9   8   7   6   5   4   3   2   1

Printed in the United States of America

Subject Reference Guide:
Woman's Suffrage – U.S. History
Woman's Rights – U.S. History
Susan B. Anthony
Alice Paul
National Woman's Party

Credits
Excerpted articles from *The New York Times, The Revolution, The Suffragist*, and other sources, credited in the text. Title page drawing from *The Suffragist*, by Nina E. Alexander, September 1920. Historic photos courtesy of National Woman's Party, pp. 44, 47, and 54. Cartoon, p. 51, Cleveland, Ohio Leader, Jan. 1917. *The Papers of Elizabeth Cady Stanton and Susan B. Anthony*, eds. Patricia G. Holland and Ann D. Gordon (Wilmington, Del.: Scholary Resources, Inc., 1989, microfilm), Series 1.

Acknowledgments
I would like to express my appreciation to the following libraries for their assistance and the use of their materials:

The Arthur and Elizabeth Schlesinger Library on the History of Women in America, Radcliffe College, Cambridge, MA

The Harry Elkins Widener Memorial Library, Harvard University, Cambridge, MA

The Daniel H. O'Leary Library, University of Massachusetts at Lowell, MA

Chelmsford Public and High School Libraries, Chelmsford, MA

East Baton Rouge Parish Library, Baton Rouge, LA

The Henry E. Huntington Library, San Marino, CA

And a special thank you to Patricia G. Holland & Susan Julian Gates.

Table of Contents

Foreword 5

Seneca Falls 8
An excerpt from Lucretia Mott: Friend of Justice
by Kem Knapp Sawyer 9
Excerpts from The Declaration of Sentiments 11
Excerpts of Resolutions Approved at Seneca Falls 13

The Long Campaign 15
Excerpts from "The Right to Vote" by Bill Severn 17
Editorial from the first issue of The Revolution 22
Report of a speech by Everett P. Wheeler 24
"Ain't I a woman?" a speech by Sojourner Truth
edited by Professor E.D. Hirsch Jr. 25
"Valentines Pour in Upon Congress" The Suffragist 27

Susan Votes 30
"The Democrat and Chronicle"
History of Women Suffrage 31
A letter written by Susan B. Anthony 31
"The Woman Franchise" The New York Times 34
Excerpts from the Diary of Susan B. Anthony 35
"Miss Susan B. Anthony Fined $100 and Costs
for Illegal Voting" The New York Times 36

Parading for Votes 38
"Suffrage Army Out on Parade" The New York Times 38
"5,000 Women March, Beset by Crowds"
The New York Times 41
"The Uprising of the Women" The New York Times 43
"Parade Protest Arouses Senate" The New York Times 46
Sheet music from The Suffragist 48

Silent Sentinels 50

"Suffragists Wait at the White House for Action"
The Suffragist 51

"On the Picket Line" a poem by Beulah Amidon 53

"Women Arrested" The Suffragist 54

"That Night of Terror" The Suffragist 55

Victory 59

"Liberation Yesterday" The New York Times 61

Bibliography 63

About the Author 64

Foreword

Forward out of error
Leave behind the night
Forward through the darkness
Forward into light

A banner bearing these words was carried by Inez Millholland Boissevain in 1910, in one of the first great parades in support of a woman's right to vote. A devoted worker for the woman's suffrage movement, she collapsed in the middle of a speech in Los Angeles in 1916. A month later she was dead. The last words she delivered in that speech rang out as a clarion call to other workers for the cause: "How long must women wait for liberty?"

In the United States the women had been waiting a very long time indeed. As far back as March 31, 1776, Abigail Adams wrote to her husband, John, saying:

". . . in the new Code of Laws. . . I desire you would Remember the Ladies, and be more generous and favourable to them than your ancestors. . . If perticuliar care and attention is not paid to the Laidies we are determined to foment a Rebelion, and will not hold ourselves bound by any Laws in which we have no voice, or Representation."

The official beginning of the "Rebelion" was at Seneca Falls, New York, on July 19 and 20, 1848. At that convention women publicly expressed dissatisfaction with their lack of legal rights. The demand for a right to vote was one of several resolutions approved by the women assembled there. The struggle to gain that right would last until 1920, when the nineteenth amendment became law.

Some of the women who worked so hard in those early years had gained their political skills in the anti-slavery movement. Many were also active in the temperance movement and were advocates for the rights of working women. At times these other movements sidetracked the women from their efforts to gain elective franchise. They suffered a great disappointment when the right to vote was given to former slaves after the Civil War but not to women. But there were also times of triumph. One of those was in 1869, when the Wyoming Territorial Legislature became the first to give female residents the right to vote.

The long struggle spanned several generations and involved women of all ages. Among the early leaders were Elizabeth Cady Stanton, Lucretia Mott, Lucy Stone, and Susan B. Anthony—none of whom would live to see the amendment pass. In the later years there were younger, college-educated women who took up the challenge: women like Carrie Chapman Catt, a master at organization, and Alice Paul, who had learned her political tactics from the more militant women of England. There were also new supporters: rich wives of the wealthy industrialists of the early twentieth century like Mrs. O.H.P. Belmont, and independently wealthy women like Mrs. Frank Leslie. In the final years, ordinary, everyday women were willing to march, speak on street corners, hand out leaflets, and even endure prison to gain the right to vote.

This book contains a collection of historical items relating to selected events in the struggle for woman's suffrage. The letters, diary entries, newspaper clippings and other articles give personality and life to the movement. There is only room to present a few of the many interesting events which took place during the 72 years of the movement. Others are available to you in the books and archives of your local library and through old periodicals.

Note: To preserve the flavor of the primary source materials in this book, original spellings, and misspellings, have been kept intact.

Seneca Falls

A short announcement in the *Seneca County Courier* on July 14, 1848, called women to Seneca Falls, New York for a convention on the rights of women. Planned on short notice, it was to be the first of several conventions held in the eastern United States that summer, and the first official step taken in the quest for woman's suffrage. It is interesting that of all the resolutions approved at Seneca Falls, only one did not have unanimous support—the resolution demanding the right to vote for women.

These conventions brought together women in different parts of the country, some of whom were already interested in women's rights and others who were merely curious. They also sparked a flurry of interesting editorials on the place of women in the social order. In the *Rochester Advertiser* one person wrote, "To us they appear extremely dull and uninteresting, and, aside from the novelty, hardly worth notice."

An editorial in the *Mechanics Advocate* in Albany, New York said:

"We are sorry to see that the women in several parts of this State are holding what they call 'Women's Rights Conventions' and setting forth a formidable list of those Rights in a parody upon the Declaration of Independence. . . . Now it requires no argument to prove that this is all wrong. Every truehearted female will instantly feel that this is unwomanly, and that to be practically carried out, the males must change their position in society to the same extent in an opposite direction, in order to enable them to discharge an equal share of the domestic duties which now appertain to females, and which must be neglected to a great extent, if women are allowed to exercise all the 'rights' that are claimed by these convention holders. . . . It would produce no positive good, that would not be outweighed tenfold by positive evil."

On the other hand, James Gordon Bennett, in *The New York Herald*, said, "We are much mistaken if Lucretia [Mott] would not make a better President than some of those who have lately tenanted the White House."

In this section you will find a description of the convention, the Declaration of Sentiments, and the Resolutions approved at Seneca Falls.

An excerpt from *Lucretia Mott: Friend of Justice*
by Kem Knapp Sawyer

"Speaking Out on Women's Rights"

In the summer of 1848, Lucretia Mott and James [Mott] traveled to New York to see several settlements of escaped slaves. They also visited with Lucretia's sister and brother-in-law, Martha and David Wright, in Auburn, New York. On this trip Lucretia once again met Elizabeth Cady Stanton and she was reminded of one of Elizabeth's letters. "The more I think on the present condition of woman, the more am I oppressed with the reality of her degradaton" she had written. "The laws of our country, how unjust are they! our customs, how vicious!" Lucretia,

Elizabeth, Lucretia's sister Martha, and two other Quakers talked over tea and together they decided to call a Woman's Rights Convention. It was to be held in the nearby town of Seneca Falls, where Elizabeth lived. A notice they placed in the *Seneca County Courier* said the convention would "discuss the social, civil, and religious conditions and rights of woman."

The organizers opened the doors to the convention at 10 a.m. on Wednesday, July 19 at the Wesleyan Chapel. Once the meeting started, Lucretia became what one observer called its "guiding spirit." Lucretia and Elizabeth had written a Declaration of Sentiments based on the Declaration of Independence, but making several key changes. They began with: "We hold these truths to be self-evident: that all men and women are created equal." The Declaration, read out loud many times during the convention, called for equal rights for women to obtain a college education, pursue a career, own property and vote. One hundred men and women signed the declaration.

Newspapers all around the nation ridiculed the Women's Rights Convention. Reporters everywhere poked fun at Lucretia Mott and Elizabeth Cady Stanton. But all the press coverage aroused readers' interest in women's rights and inspired women to hold their own conventions.

Excerpts from The Declaration of Sentiments

When, in the course of human events, it becomes necessary for one portion of the family of man to assume among the people of the earth a position different from that which they have hitherto occupied, but one to which the laws of nature and of nature's God entitle them, a decent respect to the opinions of mankind requires that they should declare the causes that impel them to such a course.

We hold these truths to be self-evident: that all men and women are created equal; that they are endowed by their Creator with certain inalienable rights; that among these are life, liberty, and the pursuit of happiness; that to secure these rights governments are instituted, deriving their just powers from the consent of the governed. Whenever any form of government becomes destructive of these ends, it is the right of those who suffer from it to refuse allegiance to it, and to insist upon the institution of a new government, laying its foundation on such principles, and organizing its powers in such form, as to them shall seem most likely to effect their safety and happiness. . . . Such has been the patient sufferance of the women under this government, and such is now the necessity which constrains them to demand the equal station to which they are entitled.

The history of mankind is a history of repeated injuries and usurpations on the part of man toward woman, having in direct object the establishment of an absolute tyranny over her. To prove this, let facts be submitted to a candid world.

He has never permitted her to exercise her inalienable right to the elective franchise.

He has compelled her to submit to laws, in the formation of which she had no voice.

He has withheld from her rights which are given to the most ignorant and degraded men—both natives and foreigners.

Having deprived her of this first right of a citizen, the elective franchise, thereby leaving her without representation in the halls of legislation, he has oppressed her on all sides.

He has made her, if married, in the eye of the law, civilly dead.

He has taken from her all right in property, even to the wages she earns. . . .

After depriving her of all rights as a married woman, if single, and the owner of property, he has taxed her to support a government which recognizes her only when her property can be made profitable to it. . . .

He has denied her the facilities for obtaining a thorough education, all colleges being closed against her. . . .

He has endeavored, in every way that he could, to destroy her confidence in her own powers, to lessen her self-respect, and to make her willing to lead a dependent and abject life.

Now, in view of this entire disfranchisement of one-half the people of this country, their social and religious degradation—in view of the unjust laws above mentioned, and because women do feel themselves aggrieved, oppressed, and fraudulently deprived of their most sacred rights, we insist that they have immediate admission to all the rights and privileges which belong to them as citizens of the United States.

In entering upon the great work before us, we anticipate no small amount of misconception, misrepresentation, and ridicule; but we shall use every instrumentality within our power to effect our object. We shall employ agents, circulate tracts, petition the State and National legislatures, and endeavor to enlist the pulpit and the press in our behalf. We hope this Convention will be followed by a series of Conventions embracing every part of the country.

Excerpts of Resolutions Approved at Seneca Falls

Resolved, That such laws as conflict, in any way, with the true and substantial happiness of woman, are contrary to the great precept of nature and of no validity, for this is "superior in obligation to any other."

Resolved, That all laws which prevent woman from occupying such a station in society as her conscience shall dictate, or which place her in a position inferior to that of man, are contrary to the great precept of nature, and therefore of no force or authority.

Resolved, That woman is man's equal—was intended to be so by the Creator, and the highest good of the race demands that she should be recognized as such.

Resolved, That the women of this country ought to be enlightened in regard to the laws under which they live, that they may no longer publish their degradation by declaring themselves satisfied with their present position, nor their ignorance, by asserting that they have all the rights they want.

Resolved, That inasmuch as man, while claiming for himself intellectual superiority, does accord to woman moral superiority, it is pre-eminently his duty to encourage her to speak and teach, as she has an opportunity, in all religious assemblies.

Resolved, That the same amount of virture, delicacy, and refinement of behavior that is required of woman in the social state, should also be required of man, and the same transgressions should be visited with equal severity on both man and woman. . . .

Resolved, That it is the duty of the women of this country to secure to themselves their sacred right to the elective franchise.

Resolved, That the equality of human rights results necessarily from the fact of the identity of the race in capabilities and responsibilities. . . .

At the last session Lucretia Mott offered and spoke to the following resolution:

Resolved, That the speedy success of our cause depends upon the zealous and untiring efforts of both men and women, for the overthrow of the monopoly of the pulpit, and for the securing to woman an equal participation with men in the various trades, professions, and commerce.

The Long Campaign

Seventy-two years separated the Seneca Falls convention and the passage of the nineteenth amendment. During those years there would be many conventions, speeches and campaigns before the final victory. For many years the efforts lacked unity and were divided by the two national groups and many state organizations. There was also a difference of opinion on whether the campaign should be a state-by-state initiative or a single push for a federal amendment. Still, there were many workers who did not give up hope during those years when the right to vote seemed always out of reach.

One example of the work done during that time is the newspaper *The Revolution*. The newspaper was first issued in January of 1868 with Elizabeth Cady Stanton and Parker Pillsbury as editors and Susan B. Anthony as proprietor. The paper lasted for three years and discussed many other woman's issues in addition to the question of the right to vote.

In 1872, Susan B. Anthony decided to respond to an editorial in her Rochester, New York newspaper which encouraged people to "Register Now." After explaining the fourteenth amendment to the young officials, Susan and her sister were allowed to register. Several friends followed her lead, and the women voted several days later in the election of November 5, 1872. However, this was not the end of the story. The women were arrested for voting illegally, and Susan's trial was held in June of 1873. At the end of the short trial the judge refused to submit the case to the jury and ordered a verdict of guilty. Susan was fined $100 which she refused to pay. She was never penalized for this and the fine was never collected.

By the beginning of the twentieth century, Susan B. Anthony and Elizabeth Cady Stanton were both in their eighties, and Lucretia Mott was dead. Susan B. Anthony recognized the need for younger women to take the lead in the movement. At the convention of the National American Woman Suffrage Association held in Washington D.C. in 1900, she brought forward Carrie Chapman Catt to be the new president. Catt's ability to organize and her talent at public speaking made her a natural leader for the new century.

In this section you will find an article giving an overview of the work done in the latter half of the nineteenth century, an editorial from the first copy of The Revolution, *some opposing opinions, a speech by Sojourner Truth at a woman's rights convention, and an interesting article about one effort aimed at congress called 'Valentines for Votes.'*

Excerpts from *The Right to Vote*
by Bill Severn

All the controversy [at Seneca Falls] started some women thinking in nearby Rochester, New York, and that same year they held a woman's rights convention there that once again brought male ridicule but also enormous publicity. Soon, without any central direction, new groups began to spring up almost everywhere, with statewide meetings in Ohio, Indiana, Pennsylvania and Kansas.

More than one thousand delegates from places as distant as California crowded into Worcester, Massachusetts, in October, 1850, for the first National Woman's Rights Convention. A central committee was organized to produce literature and help plan other conventions and resolutions were adopted that "women are clearly entitled to the right of suffrage" and that "political rights acknowledge no sex and that therefore the word 'male' should be stricken from every state constitution."

After that national conventions were held every year, state conventions were so frequent there was one somewhere every few months, and there were hundreds of smaller gatherings to swell the talk of woman's rights. Among those attracted to the movement was Susan B. Anthony, who had moved as a child with her Quaker family from Massachusetts to Rochester, New York, and who was a teacher and head of a girls' academy before she met Elizabeth Stanton and became a woman suffrage crusader.

She was a frequent visitor to the Stanton home in Seneca Falls and they became close friends and partners who planned together, wrote together, shared speaking platforms and drew up hundreds of resolutions, protests, appeals and petitions. Although there were many others who helped lead the movement, they became the driving force of its early years. Elizabeth Stanton was its philosopher and writer and Susan Anthony the one who brought it organization and political strength.

Hundreds of women were to devote a good part of their lives to the battle and they raised millions of dollars to support it through various suffrage associations. The Civil War brought a temporary halt to suffrage drives, but during the half-century that followed women organized nearly five hundred campaigns to try to change the voting laws of the states. They carried the fight into state and national political conventions, made it an issue in presidential elections, and in Washington sought action from nineteen congresses on a constitutional amendment for nationwide voting rights.

Yet the first small victory came without the help of the national associations. It was entirely a local effort by some pioneering women of the West. They quietly convinced the leaders of the first legislature of the new Territory of Wyoming that women who shared the dangers, labors and hardships of the frontier with their men deserved to share in its government.

Without petitions or any organized campaign the women of Wyoming became the first in the modern world to win the unlimited right to vote. There was some opposition but no great excitement as the territorial legislature finally passed the bill by a three-vote majority. It was signed into law December 10, 1869, and when Wyoming later applied for statehood woman suffrage was written into its new constitution.

Suffragists were a long time winning another victory in the states. In Washington their petitions to congress for nationwide voting rights by constitutional amendment were treated as a joke. It wasn't until 1878 that Susan Anthony managed to win the first senate committee hearing on the proposed amendment introduced for her that year by Senator Aaron Sargent of California, which simply and directly declared: "The right of citizens of the United States to vote shall not be denied or abridged by the United States or any state on account of sex."

What became known as the "Anthony Amendment" remained unchanged in its wording during the forty-two more years it was to take before it finally was made part of the constitution. In 1878 Elizabeth Stanton headed the women witnesses who argued for it before the Senate Committee on Privileges and Elections, whose members treated her with what she called "studied inattention and contempt." They stretched their arms, yawned in her face, stared at the ceiling, wandered away to sharpen pencils, and otherwise made it clear that the amendment had no chance of getting past the committee.

The suffragists had it introduced again at the next session of congress, and at every session after that, and hearings in one house or the other at least kept the issue alive in the newspapers. Gradually they also gained more support among members of congress. In 1882 both branches of congress appointed select committees and both favorably reported. Two years later and again in 1886 senate committees repeated their favorable reports, and the proposed amendment finally reached the senate floor for debate.

Hopes were high on January 25, 1887, when the Senate voted on woman suffrage for the first time. But the result was a crushing defeat. The Senate rejected it by a vote of more than two to one. For more than a quarter of a century, the Senate refused to vote on it again.

When they recovered from the blow the women reorganized their forces. They brought together two long-divided national groups and merged them in 1890 into a new National American Woman Suffrage Association pledged to a renewed battle in the states. Their goal was the winning of rights state by state until women voters had enough real political strength to force congress to recognize their demand for a constitutional amendment.

They turned again to the Far West. In Colorado in 1893 the woman suffrage question was put to the voters in a special referendum. Chosen to lead the battle there was Carrie Chapman Catt, long active in state suffrage campaigns. She had been an Iowa school principal and then a newspaper reporter in San Francisco before deciding to devote her life to the cause of woman's rights, and soon would head the national association when Susan Anthony retired. Carrie Chapman Catt's successful campaign in Colorado brought women their first state victory since Wyoming.

Utah and Idaho were the next to give women the vote, in 1896. After that fourteen years of battling in the states brought only defeat. But in 1910, after twice rejecting woman suffrage, the state of Washington was won over to it. Within two more years the big state of California, and then Oregon, Arizona and Kansas accepted women as voters. The tide rolled across the Mississippi in 1913 and the women of Illinois gained the vote in municipal, county and presidential elections.

The movement had grown strong, with influential supporters in state and national governments, with intelligently planned and well-financed political strategy, and with an increasing effect on public opinion everywhere. . . .

But all of it had not yet changed the minds of the men in the Congress of the United States. The proposed constitutional amendment for woman suffrage had not moved in congress since 1887, buried in committee hearings that droned on annually like respectful services for the dead.

Editorial from the first issue of *The Revolution*
New York, January 8, 1868

SALUTATORY.

A NEW paper is the promise of a new thought;
of something better or different, at least, from what
has gone before.

With the highest idea of the dignity and power of
the press, this journal is to represent no party, sect,
or organization, but individual opinion; editors and
correspondents alike, all writing, from their own
stand point, and over their own names. The enfranchisement of woman is one of the leading ideas
that calls this journal into existence. Seeing, in its
realization, the many necessary changes in our modes
of life, we think "THE REVOLUTION" a fitting name
for a paper that will advocate so radical a reform
as this involves in our political, religious and social
world.

With both man and woman in the editorial department, we shall not have masculine and feminine
ideas alone, but united thought on all questions of
national and individual interest.

But we do not promise the millennium in journal-
ism, from this experiment, or in politics from the enfranchisement of woman, only a new, and, we hope,
a better phase of existence, which, to those who are
tired of the old grooves in which the world has run
so long, is something to be welcomed in the future.
With the moral chaos that surrounds us on every
side, the corruption in the State, the dissensions in
the church, the jealousies in the home, what thinking

mind does not feel that we need something new and revolutionary in every department of life. Determined to do our part in pushing on the car of progress we begin with the new year, a new life work, hoping the world will be the better for the birth of "THE REVOLUTION."

Report of a speech by Everett P. Wheeler at a meeting held by the New York State Association Opposed to Woman Suffrage in March, 1913; taken from The New York Times.

"It is the status of the women in America under our existing system that more than anything else has made this country what it is," said Mr. Wheeler. "You see here the development of those civilizing forces which have been at work for thousands of years. You find here on the one hand that the man, the father, is the bread winner, who cares for his family, and as part of this duty elects the officers who are to perform the duties of Government. On the other hand you see mothers rearing children and bringing them up. To deprive the little child of this care and nurture is to rob the child of its dearest heritage, the heritage for which men in all the generations have struggled, prayed and toiled.

"It is upon mothers that the whole burden of future America rests, more than upon Legislatures.

"Nothing shows more clearly the failure of the suffragists, to realize the facts of the case than their favorite argument, that it is no burden to spend a few minutes putting a piece of paper in a box. If this is all they want let them set up boxes of their own and have a play election once a year.

"But, in fact, the agitation they promote, if it means anything at all, means they want a full share in civil government. If this object was attained it needs no prophet to predict that it would destroy the peace of families and that in the end it would destroy the country and the race."

'Ain't I a woman?'
Sojourner Truth fights back at convention
edited by Professor E.D. Hirsch Jr.
The Sun, February 28, 1993

Sojourner Truth was born into slavery in New York in 1795, and gained her freedom in 1827, when the state emancipated its slaves. After working as a domestic for several years, she began to speak publicly on behalf of abolition and the rights of women. In 1851, she attended a women's convention in Akron, Ohio. The convention participants did not support her attendance; they were afraid that their cause, the rights of women, would be damaged if it were associated with the rights of blacks. Sojourner Truth rose from her seat and approached the platform.
— E.D. Hirsch Jr.

Well, children, there is so much racket there must be something out of kilter. I think that 'twixt the Negroes of the South and the women of the North, all talking about rights, the white men will be in a fix pretty soon. But what's all this talking about? That man over there says that women need to be helped into carriages, and lifted over ditches, and to have the best place everywhere. Nobody helps me into carriages, or over mud puddles, or gives me any best place! Ain't I a woman? Look at me! Look at my arm! I have ploughed and planted, and gathered into barns, and no man could head me! And ain't I a woman? I could work as much and eat as much as man—when I could get it—and bear the lash as well!

And ain't I a woman? I have borne 13 children, and seen them most all sold off to slavery, and when I cried out with my mother's grief, none but Jesus heard me! And ain't I a woman?

Then they talk about this thing in my head; what's this they call it? (Intellect, someone whispers.) That's it, honey. What's that got to do with women's rights or Negroes' rights?

If my cup won't hold but a pint, and yours holds a quart, wouldn't you be mean not to let me have my half-measure full? Then that little man in black there, he says women can't have as much rights as men, 'cause Christ wasn't a woman!

From God and woman! Man had nothing to do with Him! If the first woman God ever made was strong enough to turn the world upside down all alone, these women together ought to be able to turn it back, and get it right side up again! And now they is asking to do it, the men better let them. Obliged to you for hearing me, and now old Sojourner Truth ain't got nothing more to say.

Valentines Pour in Upon Congress
Suffragists Ask Legislators to be Their Valentine, and Vote "Aye" on Susan B. Anthony Amendment
The Suffragist, February 19, 1916

On the morning of February 14, the President, the Vice-President, and the 64th Congress were again reminded of woman suffrage.

A thousand suffrage valentines were received by senators and representatives from members of the Congressional Union living in their districts. The valentines varied greatly in character, but every one conveyed the same message. It served to remind our national legislators that the Susan B. Anthony amendment is before this Congress and that hundreds of women all over the country are watchfully waiting for action. . . .

Some of the Senators who voted against the Susan B. Anthony amendment in the last Congress received yellow blotters on which were inscribed the following words: "AN OPPORTUNITY TO BLOT OUT YOUR PAST AND VOTE RIGHT THIS TIME. VOTE AYE ON THE SUSAN B. ANTHONY AMENDMENT." . . .

Representative Williams of Illinois, a member of the Judiciary Committee, is the proud possessor of three poems from his State. Mr. Webb of North Carolina, Chairman of the Judiciary, had at least half a dozen, and Mr. Carlin, a member of the committee from Virginia, was fairly showered with valentines.

One of Mr. William's verses read:

Said Congress to the ladies,
  On St. Valentine, his day,
"I'm very, very busy now,
  I wish you'd keep away."

Then said the ladies firmly,
  "Your business we note,
But we are very busy, too.
  We're working for the vote.

"And naught would please us better
  Than that business to resign,
If you'd just give us suffrage,
  For our Leap Year Valentine." . . .

Representative George W. Loft of New York received one of the cleverest of the valentines. The fact that he is a candy manufacturer gave the suffragists an unusually good opportunity. The verses sent him were:

Who is it eats your famous sweets
  By million pounds a year?
You've just one guess—we women, yes,
  Your judgment, George, is clear.
We're good enough to make you rich,
  It's now your turn at bat.
Be good enough to vote for us—
  We'll hold you, George, to that.
Put our amendment through—don't wait,
  Then you will be our candidate. . . .

Suffragists Ask Legislators to be Their Valentine, and Vote "Aye" on Susan B. Anthony Amendment

H is for HURRY —
WHICH HENRY SHOULD DO

E is for EVERY —
WHICH INCLUDES WOMEN TOO

N is for NOW —
THE MOMENT TO ACT

R is for RULES —
WHICH MUST BEND TO THE FACT

Y is for YOU —
WITH STATESMANLIKE TACT

An Acrostic for Mr. Henry, of Texas, Chairman of the Rules Committee

Susan Votes

When Susan B. Anthony saw the following editorial encouraging people to register to vote, she was stirred to action. With one of her sisters she went to their precinct office in Rochester, New York. After explaining the fourteenth amendment to the young officials, the women were allowed to register. Other friends followed their lead and the women voted a few days later in the election on November 5, 1872. However, this was not the end of the story; on Thanksgiving Day the women were arrested. The inspectors who allowed them to vote were also arrested, and later convicted.

Susan's trial was held in June, 1873, in the U.S. Circuit Court in Canandaigua, New York. At the end of a short trial Judge Ward Hunt refused to submit the case to the jury and ordered a verdict of guilty. Susan's lawyer's, Judge Henry Selden and John Van Voohris, protested but to no avail. Susan was fined $100 which she refused to pay. She was never penalized for this and the fine was never collected. The other women's cases were not brought to trial.

In this section you will find the editorial which prompted Susan B. Anthony to register to vote, two letters which she wrote, a newspaper clipping describing the trial, a page of her diary written on the date of the trial, and a letter to the editor of The New York Times *criticizing her actions.*

"The Democrat and Chronicle"
Rochester, NY
History of Women Suffrage, Volume 2, 1861-1876

Editorial of November 1, 1872

*It was on November 1st, 1872, at her quiet home
in Rochester, while reading her morning paper, that
Miss Anthony's eye fell on the following editorial:*

Now Register? To-day and to-morrow are the only
remaining opportunities. If you were not permitted
to vote, you would fight for the right, undergo all
privations for it, face death for it. You have it now at
the cost of five minutes' time to be spent in seeking
your place of registration, and having your name
entered. And yet, on election day, less than a week
hence, hundreds of you are likely to lose your votes
because you have not thought it worth while to give
the five minutes. To-day and to-morrow are your
only opportunities. Register now!

Rochester Nov. 5th 1872

Dear Mrs Stanton

Well I have been & gone & done it!! – positive-
ly voted the Republican ticket – strait – this A.M.
at 7 o clock & swore my vote in at that – was registered on Friday & 15 other women followed suit
in this ward – then in sundry others some 20 or
thirty other women tried to register, but all save two
were refused – all my three sisters voted – Rhoda

De Garmo – too – Amy Post was rejected – & she will immediately bring action against the registrars – then another woman who was registered but vote refused will bring action for that – similar to the Washington action. Hon Henry R. Selden will be our counsel – he has read up the law & all of our arguments & is satisfied that we are right & ditto the Judge Samuel Selden – his elder brother – so we are in for a fine agitation in Rochester on the question –

I hope the morning's telegrams will tell of many women all over the county trying to vote – It is splendid that without any concert of action so many should have moved here.

Thanks for the Hartford Papers. – What a magnificient meeting you had – splendid climax of the campaign – the two ablest & most eloquent women on one platform – & the Gov. of the state by your side – I was with you in spirit that evening, the Chairman of the Committee had both telegraphed & written me all about the arrangements –

Haven't we wedged ourselves into the work pretty fairly & fully – & now that the Republicans have taken our votes – for it is the Republican members of the Board – the Democratic paper is out against us strong – & that scared the Democrats on the registry board –

How I wish you were here to write of the funny things said & done – Rhoda De Garmo told them she wouldn't swear nor affirm – but would tell them the truth – & they accepted that. When the Democrats said my vote should not go in the box – one Republican said to the other – What do you say

Marsh? – I say put it in! – So do I said Jones –
and – "We'll fight it out on this live if it takes all
winter." – Mary Hollowell was just here – she &
Mrs Millis tried to register but were refused. – also
Mrs Mann the Unitarian Minister's wife – & Mary
Curtiss, – sister of Catharine Stebbins – not a jeer
not a word – not a look disrespectful has met a
single woman –

If only now – all the Woman Suffrage women
would work to this end of enforcing the existing constitution supremacy of national law over state law
– what strides we might make this very winter–
But – I'm awful tired – for five days I have been
on the constant run – but to splendid purpose –
so all right – I hope you voted too –

affectionately –
Susan B. Anthony

The Woman Franchise.

The New York Times, February 3, 1873

To the Editor of The New York Times:

May I ask you to give me space for a few words? I have this morning read Mrs. E. C. Stanton's communication on the subject of Miss Anthony's case, now before the courts, and I cannot refrain from saying a word to these ladies. Have they, while working so earnestly for the enfranchisement of women, an idea of how the majority of their countrywomen feel on the subject? I believe, from all that I have ever been able to ascertain, that for every one woman who desires to vote, there are ten at the least computation who do not wish to do so. And are we, the majority of educated women in this country, to have political duties thrust upon us, which we not only do not desire, but utterly abhor! In our hatred of publicity, in our desire to keep utterly aloof from a matter which is so distasteful to us, we have said too little, have kept silence too long, until the strong-minded party think we care nothing about it. Could I speak with a thousand tongues, it would be to give a hundred thousand reasons why we should not vote. We can use our influence in our homes, a woman's proper sphere, and who can tell how much we do use it now! It is all we want. Let almost any woman who has a family to care for speak, and say how much time she has to devote to the study of political questions, and to the duties which are incumbent upon voters; for if we are made voters, we are in honor bound to fulfill to the utmost all the duties attached to the so-called "privilege." . . . To the women of our land who yet love their own womanly sphere, I say, Keep silence in public when you can; but work, work at home in your own dominion, that we may be saved from this fate. I hope, and I know that I speak for many besides myself in saying this, that for many years to come there may be found men enough who care for the peace, dignity, modesty, and womanly reserve of their mothers, wives, daughters, and sisters to protect us from having thrust upon us that dreaded "right" of voting.

A Woman.

No. 461 West Twenty-third-Street, New-York, Thursday, Jan. 30, 1873.

Excerpts from the Diary of Susan B. Anthony

June   Wednesday, 18   1873

Circuit Court – Judge Hunt refused Judge S. to address Jury – & instructed Jury to bring in verdict of guilty – & refused to poll jury – Inspector's convicted & Van Voorhis denied address to jury – The greatest outrage history ever witnessed –

June   Thursday, 19

Mrs Hebbard, Mosher, Leyden, Anthony, Pulver came down to Cand. – New trial moved by both Selden & Van V. – hearing at 2. P.M. – masterly statements of cause by both S. & V. – Judge H. denied my case at once – deferred Inspectors till morning – Att. moved my sentence – Judge asked reason why sentence should not be. I answered –

I have much to say – A sublime silence reigned in court while I declared every right stricken down –

June Friday, 20

Mrs Gage went home – & so did I – but Friday A.M. found me in court again, bound to stand by & see the Inspectors through. V's pleas were clear & unanswerable but no law, logic or justice could change his will. We were convicted before hearing & all trial a mere farce –

Miss Susan B. Anthony Fined $100 and
Costs for Illegal Voting.
The New York Times, June 20, 1873

CANANDAIGUA, N.Y., June 19.—At 2 o'clock this afternoon Judge Selden made a motion in the case of Miss Anthony for a new trial, upon the ground of a misdirection of the judge in ordering a verdict of guilty without submitting the case to the jury. He maintained, in an elaborate argument, the right of every person charged with crime to have the question of guilt or innocence passed upon by a constitutional jury, and that there was no power in this court to deprive her of it.

The District Attorney replied, when the Court, in a brief review of the argument of the counsel, denied the motion.

The District Attorney immediately moved that the judgment of the Court be pronounced upon the defendant.

The Court made the usual inquiry of Miss Anthony if she had anything to say why sentence should not be pronounced.

Miss Anthony answered and said she had a great many things to say, and declared that in her trial every principle of justice had been violated; that every right had been denied; that she had had no trial by her peers; that the Court and the jurors were her political superiors and not her peers, and announced her determination to continue her labors until equality was obtained, and was proceeding to discuss the question involved in the case, when she was interrupted by the Court with the remark that these questions could not be reviewed.

Miss Anthony replied she wished it fully understood that she asked no clemency from the Court; that she desired and demanded the full rigor of the law.

Judge Hunt then said the judgment of the Court is that you pay a fine of $100 and the costs of the prosecution, and immediately added, there is no order that you stand committed until the fine is paid; and so the trial ended.

A motion for a new trial is to be made in the case of the inspectors to-morrow morning on the ground that Hall, one of the defendants, was absent during the trial.

Parading for Votes

In the last decade of the fight for women's suffrage, 1910-1920, a new tactic was used to bring the subject of votes for women to the attention of the nation. Huge parades were held in many cities, beautifully planned events with floats, banners, women on horseback, and music, all demonstrating the conviction of the marchers that women deserved the right to vote. In one parade on May 22, 1910, ninety automobiles took part. *The New York Times* noted that two cars were not only driven by women, but they were also the women's "own machines." Many parades passed peacefully; a few did not. They did bring a great deal of notice to the cause.

In this section you will find descriptions of several parades, including one in Washington where women were treated very roughly. You will also find an editorial written after one of the New York parades, and a piece of music written for the woman's movement.

Suffrage Army Out On Parade
The New York Times, May 5, 1912: pg. 1

Ten thousand strong, the army of those who believe in the cause of woman's suffrage marched up Fifth Avenue at sundown yesterday in a parade the like of which New York never knew before. Dusty and weary, the marchers went to their homes last night satisfied that their year of hard work in preparing for the demonstration had borne good fruit.

It was an immense crowd that came out to stand upon the sidewalks to cheer or jeer. . . . It was a crowd that took every inch of the sidewalk from Washington Square to Carnegie Hall, that filled all the steps and crowded all the windows along the line of march. . . .

The Start of the Parade.

Promptly at 5 o'clock. . . the order to start the parade came. . . . Then a company of women on horseback trotted smartly around the east side of Washington Arch, and the great suffrage parade had begun. . . .

It took the entire line one hour and fifty-five minutes to pass. . . .

Sharp Contrasts Among the Marchers

It was a parade of contrasts—contrasts among women. There were women of every occupation and profession, and women of all ages, from those so advanced in years that they had to ride in carriages down to suffragettes so small that they were pushed along in perambulators. There were women whose faces bore traces of a life of hard work and many worries. There were young girls, lovely of face and fashionably gowned. There were motherly looking women, and others with the confident bearing obtained from contact with the business world.

There were women who smiled in a preoccupied way as though they had just put the roast into the

oven, whipped off their aprons and hurried out
to be in the parade. They were plainly worried at
leaving their household cares for so long, yet they
were determined to show their loyalty to the cause.
There were women who marched those weary miles
who had large bank accounts. There were slender
girls, tired after long hours of factory work. There
were nurses, teachers, cooks, writers, social workers,
librarians, school girls, laundry workers. There were
women who work with their heads, and women
who work with their hands, and women who never
work at all. And they all marched for suffrage. . . .

The Men's Division.

But the real excitement, the real moment in the
parade, for which many of the spectators had waited
since noon, was the delegation of men. If there were
women of every sort, there were men of every sort,
and their number, grown tremendously from the
scanty and much-derided eighty of last year, was
close to a thousand. Some said that there were more
than two thousand, but these estimates were much
too large. There were men with gray hair, who
lifted their silk hats with an old-school courtliness
in response to the chorus from the sidewalk which
bewildered them, and which they did not exactly
understand. There were young men fashionably
dressed, and some men of prominence in the city
who swung into the parade yesterday. . . .

Women Mostly Dressed in White.

Most of the women, particularly the younger
women, were dressed all in white, except for the

outflashing of yellow and purple and green and red that was in the ribbons they wore, the banners they carried, and the flags they waved. And many of the women wore the suffrage hat, trimmed to suit their own taste. . . . There were women, too, in great numbers who came in their regular street dress or gowned as they were when they quit work, to march for the cause.

Children Cheer Their Teachers.

The teachers, followed by pretty school girls innumerable, joined the parade from Washington Square. . . . Their banners commented caustically on the illiteracy of children under the rule of man. . . . And from the sidewalks there was a running chorus of amusement and delight as the school children caught sight of their teachers in the line of march. . . .

5,000 Women March, Beset by Crowds
Demonstration at Capital Badly Hampered and Congress Is Asked to Investigate.
The New York Times, March 4, 1913: pg. 5

Special to *The New York Times*

WASHINGTON. March 3.—In a woman's suffrage demonstration to-day the capital saw the greatest parade of women in its history. In the allegory presented on the Treasury steps it saw a wonderful series of dramatic pictures. In the parade over 5,000 women passed down Pennsylvania Avenue. Some were riding, more were afoot. Floats throughout the procession illustrated the progress the woman's suffrage cause had made in the last seventy-five years. Scattered throughout the parade were the standards of nearly every State in the Union. It was an astonishing demonstration.

It was estimated by Gen. John A. Johnson, a Commissioner of the District of Columbia, that 500,000 persons watched the women march for their cause. Imagine a Broadway election night crowd, with half the shouting and all of the noise-making novelties lacking; imagine that crowd surging forward constantly, without proper police restraint, and one gains some idea of the conditions that existed along Pennsylvania Avenue. . . .

. . . It was when the head of the procession turned by the great Peace Monument and started down Pennsylvania Avenue that the first indication of trouble came. Hearing the bands strike up, the crowds on both sides of the avenue pushed into the roadway. At once the police authorities knew that they had not made proper plans for keeping the spectators in restraint. . . .

. . . Through all the confusion and turmoil the women paraders marched calmly, keeping a military formation as best they could. The bands played and hundreds of yellow banners fluttered in the wind. The marchers smiled to their friends. The taunts of the curious they disregarded. . . . Miss Milholland was an imposing figure in a white broadcloth Cossack suit and long white-kid boots. From her shoulders hung a pale-blue cloak, adorned with a golden maltese cross. She was mounted on Gray Dawn, a white horse belonging to A. D. Addison of this city. Miss Milholland was by far the most picturesque figure in the parade. . . .

. . . Confusion, cheers and jeers were the order of the day until the tired marchers disbanded. For a distance of a few blocks near the end the women marched without trouble, for a squad of the Fifteenth Cavalry rode to their assistance. A band of boy scouts also did good service. . . .

. . . At one time at the height of the disorder Miss Inez Milholland helped to restrain the spectators by riding her horse into the crowd.

The Uprising of the Women.
The New York Times, May 5, 1912: pg. 14

The parade on Fifth Avenue last evening of possibly 10,000 women of various ages, many of them young and personable, all surely representative of good types of womanhood. . . . will be discussed from various points of view. Most of the comment it provokes will be humorous but amiable. Men generally view the woman suffrage movement calmly, seeming not to care much whether or not the women get the right to vote, and heeding little the consequences of the social revolution which would result from the triumph of the present agitation. . . .

The situation is dangerous. We often hear the remark nowadays that women will get the vote if they try hard enough and persistently, and it is true that they will get it, and play havoc with it for them-

Demonstration outside the White House gates.

Suffragettes parade in the nation's capitol (1913).

selves and society, . . . if the men are not firm and wise enough and, it may as well be said, masculine enough to prevent them. . . .

Granted the suffrage, they would demand all that the right implies. It is not possible to think of women as soldiers and sailors, police patrolmen, or firemen, although voters ought to fight if need be, but they would serve on juries and elect themselves if they could to executive offices and Judgeships. Many of them are looking forward to an apportionment of high offices between the sexes. This may seem preposterous to some of the men who choose to smile complacently at the aggressiveness of the women's rights adherents, but it is true. It is a state of things these men will have to cope with before they die if they do not arouse themselves and do their duty now. . . .

In her pursuit of all the privileges and duties of men, however, she is deliberately endangering many rights she now enjoys. . .

It will be a sad day for society when woman loses the respect she now receives from all but the basest of men. Yet yesterday's parade demonstrates that she holds male courtesy in slight regard, or would, if we were willing to regard the parade as a demonstration of the feelings and opinions of all our women.

Millions of men labor all their years to keep up a home, of which a woman is mistress. . . . But with the opportunity afforded to him by the refusal of woman to recognize his manhood as a title of supremacy in the world's affairs, he will be at pains to avoid some of the troubles which he has hitherto regarded as part of his heritage. . . .

There were, at most, 10,000 women in yesterday's parade. If their cause triumphs there will be 700,000 women voters in this municipality. Have the 10,000 thought much about the measure of influence they would exert if the whole number voted under the control of their associations and environment and as their intelligence impelled them to?

Parade Protest Arouses Senate
The New York Times, March 5, 1913: pg. 8

WASHINGTON. March 4.—Bitter complaint was heard on every hand to-day because of the lack of protection given to the women marchers by the Metropolitan Police during the suffrage pageant and procession yesterday. Congress had passed a special resolution directing that Pennsylvania Avenue be kept clear for the demonstration. . . . Many persons were injured.

The stories of the police do not agree. One policeman said yesterday that the police authorities had no idea that they would have to handle the tremendous crowd, equal to any inauguration gathering that flocked into Pennsylvania Avenue yesterday and had not detailed enough men for that reason. Leaders in the suffrage cause say that those policemen who were detailed did not perform their duty: . . .

"I do not want to be unfair," said Mrs. Glenna S. Tinnan of Washington, the director of the pageant, "but the treatment accorded us was simply unspeakable. It was more than a question of an undermanned police line. Those who were assigned to the task not only did little or nothing, but even seemed to encourage the hoodlums in the work of breaking up the parade." . . .

"Only one policeman that I saw did his full duty. Some stood in groups and twiddled their fingers and repeated again and again, 'We can do nothing with this crowd.' I heard another policeman say, 'If my wife were in that line of march I'd knock her down.' . . .

"The Boy Scouts," said Miss Alice Paul of Philadelphia. "were the only ones who did any effective police work."

© Harris & Ewing from Paul Thompson

Miss Alice Paul, Chairman of the National Woman's Party, celebrating the suffrage victory at her headquarters in Washington.

THE MARCH OF THE WOMEN.

ETHEL SMYTH, Mus. Doc.

PIANO.

Shout, shout, up with your song! Cry with the wind, for the

dawn is break - ing; March, march, swing you a - long,

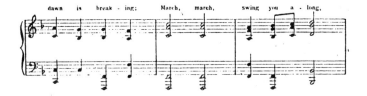

Wide blows our ban - ner, and hope is wa - king. Song with its sto - ry,

dreams with their glo - ry Lo! they call, and glad is their word!

Shout, shout, up with your song!
　　Cry with the wind, for the dawn is breaking;
March, march, swing you along,
　　Wide blows our banner, and hope is waking.
Song with its story, dreams with their glory
　　Lo! they call, and glad is their word!
Loud and louder it swells,
　　Thunder of freedom, the voice of the Lord!

Comrades—ye who have dared
　　First in the battle to strive and sorrow!
Scorned, spurned—nought have ye cared,
　　Raising your eyes to a wider morrow.
Ways that are weary, days that are dreary,
　　Toil and pain by faith ye have borne;
Hail hail—victors ye stand,
　　Wearing the wreath that the brave have worn!

Life, strife—these two are one,
　　Naught can ye win but by faith and daring.
On, on—that ye have done
　　But for the work of to-day preparing.
Firm in reliance, laugh a defiance,
　　(Laugh in hope, for sure is the end)
March, march—many as one,
　　Shoulder to shoulder and friend to friend.

49

Silent Sentinels

By 1914 the more traditional National American Woman Suffrage Association had split with a group of women, led by Alice Paul, who believed that they should hold whichever party was in power responsible for passing the woman's suffrage amendment. This group became the National Woman's Party, and in 1917 began a campaign of peacefully picketing outside the White House, a right they were assured was legal. Many of the signs displayed President Wilson's own words about democracy.

For the first few months the women were allowed to picket peacefully; however, attitudes changed after the U.S. entered World War I in April. In June, after a banner addressed to a visiting official from Russia was deemed an embarrassment, the women began to be arrested for obstructing traffic. Before this sad chapter was over, women had been sent to the Occoquan Workhouse, forcibly fed, and, in Alice Paul's case, even put in a ward for the insane.

On November 27 and 28, 1917, all of the women were suddenly released. Some of the women appealed their original sentences, and in March, 1918, it was decided that there had been no just cause to arrest the women. Since all of the pickets had been arrested on the same charge, all of the arrests were therefore invalid. For that reason the District of Columbia was ordered to bear all of the costs of the trials.

This section includes descriptions of the picketing and the imprisonment, some poetry that grew out of the movement, and some opinions generated by the picketing.

The Cut Direct

Suffragists Wait at the White House for Action
The Suffragist, January 17, 1917

There is a royal blaze of color at the White House gates these nipping winter days. Across Lafayette Square, through the lovely tracery of bare trees, the cold classic lines of the White House have receded into their winter background. Instead a gallant display of purple, white and gold banners through the trees holds the eye. They are like trumpet calls. Many were caught by the lovely sight last week when the suffrage pickets of the Congressional Union first went on guard at the White House. For the first time in history the President of these United States is being picketed, is being waited upon day after day by representatives of the women of the nation, is being asked a question that must finally be answered to the nation.

Many walked across Lafayette Square the day the banners first called, to look at the unusual sight in front of that dignified place that is each day visited by people from every part of the country. Flanking the impressive east and west gates of the White House were merely twelve young women, holding high floating purple, white and gold banners. The young women were demure and unsmiling and silent. . . .

. . . the questions that those lettered banners are day after day asking, men and women are echoing and re-echoing across the nation. "Mr. President, what are you going to do about woman's suffrage?" "Mr. President, how long must women wait for liberty?" The fact is that thousands of men and women of this nation because of those silent sentinels with their purple, white and gold standards, have asked themselves for the first time, "What is the President doing about federal suffrage? What could he do? Why is he not doing it?" From every section of the country these voices of the great rank and file that make public opinion are being expressed in the press of the country. Never before has a picket organized to call attention to a wrong excited more comment, resounded over farther territory.

On the Picket Line
by Beulah Amidon
The Suffragist, March 3, 1917

The avenue is misty gray,
And here beside the guarded gate
We hold our golden blowing flags
And wait.

The people pass in friendly wise;
They smile their greeting where we stand
And turn aside to recognize
The just demand.

Often the gates are swung aside:
The man whose power could free us now
Looks from his car to read our plea—
And bow.

Sometimes the little children laugh;
The careless folk toss careless words,
And scoff and turn away, and yet
The people pass the whole long day
Those golden flags against the gray
And can't forget.

Women picketing outside the White House.

Women Arrested
The Suffragist

Sixteen women, representing the states of the West, the East and the South, during the past week have been arrested for the peace-picketing of the White House. Beginning with a riot which was precipitated by the action of the police, the grotesque chapter which this week adds to the fifty-years' battle for suffrage will baffle future students of the movement in this country. . . .

. . . The picket went out as usual Friday, June 22, when Miss Lucy Burns and Miss Katherine Morey stood at the lower gates of the White House with the familiar banner carrying the President's own words:

"We will fight for the things we have always held nearest our hearts, for democracy, for the right of those who submit to authority to have a voice in their own governments."

For seven minutes the police pondered. "We can't arrest the President's message," they said, "they've had it out before." Then they took a chance and obeyed orders. Technically Miss Burns and Miss Morey found they were arrested for "obstructing traffic," though there had been no traffic at the time of their arrest, and Inspector Grant and Major Pullman seemed embarrassed and unable to explain the new ruling.

"That Night of Terror," November 14, 1917
As Described by Mrs. Mary A. Nolan
The Suffragist, December 1, 1917

I was giving all my time to Red Cross work in the surgical department of the Jacksonville (Florida) Branch when I first heard of Alice Paul—that they had put her in prison with those others. They were suffering and fighting for all of us. When Mrs. Gould and Miss Younger asked Florida women to go to Washington to help, I volunteered. I am seventy-three, but except for my lame foot I was well. . . .

I picketed three times with these splendid women, carrying a purple, white and gold suffrage flag. The third time we spent the night in the House of Detention because we refused to give bail. . . .

They ran through that "trial" rapidly the next day. We did not answer them or pay any attention. We knew, of course, that we would all be convicted and sentenced for months, just as the hundred and more other women who had done this thing for suffrage. . . .

It was about half past seven at night when we got to Occoquan workhouse. A woman was standing behind a desk when we were brought into this office, and there were six men also in the room. Mrs. Lewis, who spoke for all of us, refused to talk to the woman—who, I learned, was Mrs. Herndon —and said she must speak to Mr. Whittaker, the superintendent of the place. . . .

Suddenly the door literally burst open and Whittaker rushed in like a tornado; some men followed him. We could see the crowds of them on the porch. They were not in uniform. They looked as much like tramps as anything. They seemed to come in—and in—and in. One had a face that made me think of orang-outang. Mrs. Lewis stood up—we had been sitting and lying on the floor; we were so tired but she had hardly began to speak, saying we demanded to be treated as political prisoners when Whittaker said:

"You shut up! I have men here glad to handle you. Seize her!" I just saw men spring toward her and some one screamed, "They have taken Mrs. Lewis," when a man sprang at me, and caught me by the shoulder. I am used to being careful of my bad foot and I remember saying, "I'll come with you; don't drag me; I have a lame foot." But I was jerked down the steps and away into the dark. I didn't have my feet on the ground; I guess that saved me. . . .

We were rushed into a large room that we found opened on a long hall with brick dungeons on each side. "Punishment cells" is what they call them. They are dungeons. Mine was filthy; it had no window save a little slit at the top and no furniture but a sheet-iron bed and an open toilet flushed from outside the cell. . . .

I saw Dorothy Day brought in. She is a very slight girl. The two men were twisting her arms above her head. Then suddenly they lifted her up and banged her down over the arm of an iron bench—twice. As they ran me past she was lying there with her arms out, and I heard one of the men yell, "The ___ suffrager!" My mother ain't no suffrager. I'll put you through ___ ." . . .

The door was barred from top to bottom. The walls were brick cemented over. It was bitter cold. Mrs. Cosu would not let me lie on the floor. She put me on the couch and stretched out on the floor. We had only lain there a few minutes trying to get our breath when Mrs. Lewis, doubled over and handled like a sack of something, was literally thrown in by two men. Her head struck the iron bed as she fell.

We thought she was dead. She didn't move. We were crying over her as we lifted her to the bed and stretched her out, when we heard Miss Burns call: "Where is Mrs. Lewis?"

Mrs. Cosu called out, "They've just thrown her in here." We were roughly told by the guard not to dare speak again, or we would be put in straight-jackets. We were so terrified we kept very still. Mrs. Lewis was not unconscious; she was only stunned. But Mrs. Cosu was desperately ill as the night wore on. She had a bad heart attack, and then vomiting. We called and called. We asked them to send our doctor because we thought she was dying; there was a woman guard and a man in the corridor, but they paid no attention. A cold wind blew in on us from the outside, and we all lay there shivering and only half conscious until early morning. . . .

I was released on the sixth day, and passed the dispensary as I came out. There were a group of my friends, Mrs. Brannan and Mrs. Morey and several others. They had on coarse striped dresses and big grotesque heavy shoes. I burst into tears as they led me away, my term having expired. I didn't want to desert them like that, but I had done all I could.

Victory

After the Anthony Amendment was first introduced to the United States Congress on January 10, 1878, it was re-submitted many times throughout the end of the nineteenth and the beginning of the twentieth centuries, but never with success. Victory seemed near when the House of Representatives approved the amendment on January 10, 1918; however, when the Senate failed to agree, women were once again denied the right to vote.

By that time support for the amendment was beginning to grow even in some of the more conservative sections of the country. Also, women were beginning to ask for a voice in other aspects of their lives. In 1918, women asked the annual convention of the Protestant Episcopal Church in Massachusetts for the right to vote on the convention floor. After a heated dispute, the request was denied.

When the new congress convened in May of 1919, women once again faced the task of convincing congressmen to vote in favor of equal suffrage for women. Even President Woodrow Wilson cabled congress from Europe, encouraging them to approve the amendment. "It seems to me that every consideration of justice and of public advantage calls for the immediate adoption of that amendment and its submission forthwith to the legislatures of the several states."

The Anthony Amendment was again approved by the House of Representatives on May 21, 1919. This time the Senate approved the amendment on June 4. Looking back at that day, Maude Younger, who was in the Senate gallery, commented: "This was the day toward which women had been struggling for more than a half a century! We were in the dawn of woman's political power in America."

After a frantic campaign to get it ratified by two-thirds of the states, Tennessee became the final state needed for ratification on August 18, and it was signed by Governor Roberts on August 24. Although some members of the Tennessee legislature tried to get the decision annulled, Connecticut soon followed assuring the necessary states. U.S. Secretary of State Colby signed it into law on August 26, 1920, ending 72 years of struggle.

Although it was not signed in the presence of any of those women who had worked so hard to see it passed, celebrations did follow the final approval. Alice Paul celebrated with her co-workers at the head-quarters of the National Woman's Party in Washington. Carrie Chapman Catt was met in New York by cheering crowds, brass bands, and a parade up Fifth Avenue. As for the organizations formed to achieve the goal, the National American Woman Suffrage Association soon dissolved into the League of Woman Voters; the National Women's Party is still active.

Liberation Yesterday
by Marylin Bender
The New York Times, August 21, 1970

. . . the past contains the unresolved question of the future. Is the women's rights movement destined to continue as the greatest talkathon of modern times or will it achieve the transformation of modern society and the genuine equality between the sexes that has been its constant goal?

From Lucretia Mott to Betty Friedan, feminists have been indefatigably verbal. Everything said today has indeed been said and written before:

In 1837, Susan B. Anthony, then a 17-year-old teacher, was asking for equal pay for women teachers, coeducation and higher education for women.

In 1848, Elizabeth Cady Stanton and other abolitionist women assembled at Seneca Falls, N.Y., and asserted in a declaration of principles that "all men and women are equal." . . .

"Radical reform" was what Miss Anthony and Mrs. Stanton expected their magazine, The Revolution, to further in 1868. "Educated suffrage, irrespective of sex or color; equal pay to women for equal work; eight hours labor; abolition of standing armies and party despotism. Down with politicans—Up with the people!" they asked in language that seems startingly contemporary.

But then feminism has always seemed visionary. It has always swung from revolution to reaction, propelled on spasmodic bursts of energy toward astonishing achievement before subsiding into compromise and indifference. . . .

It always had its separatists, starting with Lucy Stone, who kept her name after marrying Henry Blackwell in 1855 in a remarkable ceremony that contravened all of the legal obligations of the nuptial rite. . . . There were always the militants and the conservatives, the radicals and the reformers, the single-minded suffragists and broad-gauge social reconstructionists. . . . Because of the bitter rivalry between Alice Paul and Carrie Chapman Catt, neither witnessed the signing of the suffrage proclamation. The suffrage triumph was a landmark for decline. Many feminists, old and new, acknowledged that counterrevolution followed.

A Selected Bibliography

Books

Adams, Mildred. *The Right To Be People*. New York; J.B. Lippincott Company, 1966.

Butterfield, L.H. *Adams Family Correspondence*. Cambridge, MA: The Belknap Press, 1963.

DuBois, Ellen Carol. *Feminism and Suffrage, The Emergence of an Independent Women's Movement in America, 1848-1869*. Ithaca: Cornell University Press, 1978.

Irwin, Inez Haynes. *The Story of Alice Paul And The National Woman's Party*. Fairfax: Denlinger's Publishers, Ltd., 1977.

Hahn, Emily. *Once Upon a Pedestal*. New York: Thomas Y. Crowell Company, 1974.

Harper, Ida Husted. *Life and Work of Susan B. Anthony*. New York: Arno Press, Inc., 1969.

Holland, Patricia G. and Ann D. Gordon, Eds. *The Papers of Elizabeth Cady Stanton and Susan B. Anthony*. Wilmington, DE: Scholarly Resources Inc., 1989, Microfilm.

Severn, Bill. *The Right To Vote*. New York: Ives Washburn, Inc., 1972.

Stanton, Elizabeth Cady, Susan B. Anthony, Matilda Joslyn Gage, and Ida H. Harper, Eds. *History of Woman Suffrage*. New York: Arno Press, Inc., 1969.

Van Voris, Jacqueline. *Carrie Chapman Catt, A Public Life*. New York: The Feminist Press at the City University of New York, 1987.

Woman's Rights Conventions: Seneca Falls & Rochester, 1848. New York: Arno Press, Inc., 1969.

Newspapers

"State Times," Baton Rouge, LA.

"New York Times," New York.

"The Revolution," New York: 1868-1872.

"The Suffragist," Washington, DC: 1913-1921.

About the Author

With a background in library science and social studies education, Madeleine Meyers finds researching specific events in history both fascinating and fun. "As a former school media specialist, I tried to find books with the interesting details of history that will get students involved in the social sciences. Now I have the enjoyment of searching through old newspapers and histories to produce books that I hope will fill the need."

Ms. Meyers lives in New England with her husband and two sons. She has a fascinating job in the library of an observatory where she works with a group of scientists who are looking into the far reaches of space. Through her work she has encountered a new world to explore. "I love getting on the computer and travelling through the Internet. For me it's just as fascinating as looking back in time." She also enjoys reading, travelling, gardening, and writing. Ms. Meyers has written a weekly newspaper column on local history, and is presently working on two novels.